MENTORS
MATTER

Work while they sleep,
Learn while they play,
Invest while they spend,
Pursue while they procrastinate,
and you'll live like they dream.

— **Ray Orr**
Leadership Mentor

MENTORS MATTER

A PRACTICAL GUIDE
FOR MENTORS ON THE ROLE AND RESPONSIBILITIES OF A TRUSTED ADVISOR

TAMMY KLING

and

TONY JEARY

The RESULTS Guy™

RESULTS
FASTER!

PUBLISHING

MENTORS MATTER

A practical guide for mentors on the role and responsibilities of a trusted advisor

Published by Results Faster Publishing
in Flower Mound, TX

Printed in the United States of America

CONTENTS

"One great mentor, can change your life forever."

INTRODUCTION

A great mentor will transform lives.
Not just with encouragement, but with theory and ideas that prompt psychological transformation.

A mentor will ignite the spark of creativity and hope within—either by example or in conversation.

As we set out to create this book, I thought about my early mentors, who were not coaches but were leaders of companies or large organizations, and who transformed my life with a simple conversation.

Often it was just one concept that I couldn't stop thinking about, even after months of conversations.

Concepts like Transparent Leadership, Action, or Control the Controllables, and learning new theory on blind spots and eliminating distraction.

I mentor several university students and executives; and one client, the vice president of a major company, is someone whom I've coached for seven years. The time frame of your conversations and experiences together, if you're a mentor, may be weeks, months, or years; and regardless of how long it is, you can make an impact.

A mentor will ignite the spark of creativity and hope within— either by example or in conversation.

Words are currency—that is my trademark. It's a term I created, but I also gave a TEDx talk on this topic and I believe nothing could be more true. You can change a life with your words or you can destroy a life with your words. Words have created wars, built relationships, started companies, and landed jobs.

Words change lives!

The day I first met Tony, a motivational speaker, investor, and strategist, I realized that his energy was contagious!

"I heard you work with big CEO's," he said, rolling up in his five-star golf cart to meet me at my mailbox. We both lived in Tour 18, a gated community on a golf course not far from DFW airport in Texas.

"I'm your neighbor, Tony, and I'd like to see how we can work together." He handed me a book he had written, and we arranged to schedule a meeting.

One of the first things he talked about, was strategic acceleration, and the process of production before perfection.

Just this one concept of acceleration, transformed my thinking and my business. I was able to create books with leaders, and companies—condensing the timeframe from six to nine months down to under three. And I was able to do it, focused on the same exact perfectionism that most professional authors have, simply because I eliminated all of the overthinking.

As a leader, we can get bogged down in our own chaotic thoughts; but when you decide to be committed to action, that tends to go away.

I've introduced Tony to leaders and vice versa, and we've worked on several projects together.

> *As a leader, we can get bogged down in our own chaotic thoughts; but when you decide to be committed to action, that tends to go away.*

We decided to coach each other every December prior to the new year and review goals. In those specific mentoring sessions, we've reviewed our vision boards and written goals for the new year for our businesses, kids, and family.

Mentorship is a gift. Both for the one being mentored and for the mentor as well. A mentor is able to share wisdom and knowledge about a specific topic and often many topics because they have a series of strategic thinking traits that are naturally inherent.

You don't have to know everything; you just have to guide them to more clarity.

Often times a mentor will be someone who has a God-given gift of wisdom and discernment and the ability to unravel complex problems and offer solutions that others can't see. A mentor is someone you can share things with and walk away with clarity.

> *You don't have to know everything; you just have to guide them to more clarity.*

When Tony and I first met, I was coaching CEO's through books, and I had just finished

xiv | MENTORS MATTER

writing *The Transparent Leader* with Herb Baum, the CEO of Dial Corporation. We wrote it with the understanding that it would assist in selling the company by highlighting the strong values that had built that culture.

A mentor is someone you can share things with and walk away with clarity.

Herb was one of my very first mentors, and he taught me the power of transparency. I wasn't looking for a mentor; but he asked me to help him write his book, and I did.

During that process, my entire thinking was transformed. Little did I know that it would create a domino effect where I passed on what I had learned from him to my kids, their friends, other parents, and the clients I coached and mentored.

One of the most powerful theories I learned during that season was the power of transparency, which meant living your life as if your actions were being viewed in the media. Transparency led our family to create the same passwords on every phone, which still exists 20 years later. When you are transparent and you lead with transparency, you are telling your children, your spouse, and your employees or colleagues that you have nothing to hide.

When you are transparent and you lead with transparency, you are telling your children, your spouse, and your employees or colleagues that you have nothing to hide.

It gives them a solid foundation to build their own leadership lifestyle from, and it helps them actually walk the talk instead of just talking about their core values.

And this is the way mentorship should work.

After a year of flying back-and-forth from Dallas to Dial headquarters in Arizona to work on Herb's book, I sold the manuscript to Harper Collins.

We received a six figure advance!

His team member came to me shortly after and said; "Herb would like to give you the entire advance. Where can we send the money?"

Sure enough, a $100,000 check arrived in the mail. He didn't take one dime of it and he simply gave it to me out of an act of kindness.

He really was unique.

During the process of writing the book, I had worked with his Director of Investor Relations and an entire team at Dial. Each one provided their input on stories about Herb and his leadership style, which was to be face-to-face with the people as well as hands-on. One of the most memorable stories was about an employee who was on his smoke break and called Herb's office about a dead bird outside the door of the company.

Instead of calling the janitorial staff or asking the employee why he was calling the CEO with such a trivial matter, Herb walked down, found the side door, went outside, and picked up the dead bird and threw it away.

I learned so much about character through my interactions with him, and I always strive to be like Herb.

His mentorship, although it was brief, is a perfect example of the way a mentor's words and theory should impact a life.

Mentorship isn't just about encouragement.

It's about leaving someone with a profound or divergent theory that truly can impact their lives forever.

Prior to working with Herb, I met Warren Buffett, whom I also learned so much from. I learned to buy low, and sell high. That one simple concept applies to everything in life and can transform your thinking—not just about stocks, but about real estate, about selling simple items, and about any kind of product that you create. I read several of his annual reports after that and continued to for years. In the annual reports are words of wisdom, and I passed on those reports to my children to read when they were growing up.

What's your story?

Never underestimate the power of your life experiences and the way in which sharing them will benefit someone else.

Iron sharpens iron, and there are moments when we can help someone think differently, even if they are already ultra successful. Since the beginning of time, kings, queens, and world leaders have sought out wisdom from anointed individuals who can help them change lives.

—Tammy Kling

HOW TO READ
THIS BOOK
Tony Jeary

After years of mentoring others, and coaching companies to achieve greatness and extraordinary results, I have learned a few things.

One of the things I've learned is that a great leader will always leave an individual employee better than they were when they started. You can look at someone's employees and see how great the leader is by their attitude, and also by results.

As the old saying goes, success leaves clues.

When Tammy asked me for my wisdom on co-creating this book, it wasn't hard to think of my decades of experience coaching leaders.

But this book isn't about me, it's about you. And for that reason, I want to help you become a better version of yourself when you lead and mentor others.

As the old saying goes, success leaves clues.

In the book *Uncommon Friends*, collaborative relationships are explored throughout the course of history, highlighting people like Thomas Edison, Henry Ford and others.

I would encourage you to grab a copy of this book in order to become a better mentor and understand how relationships can truly transform others.

The best way to use this book is to think of it as a mentor for mentors. This book is a living tool and a guide that we've created after years of working with leaders at the highest levels.

If you're a mentor or a mentee, remember that action and results are two of the best tools you can use to leverage your relationship success. One of the ways you can validate the relationship when you want them to pour into you more, is to make sure you report in to them that you've taken action and you're appreciating that insight.

It's not just about their ego; it's about offering up gratitude for their time and wisdom.

Remember, even if your mentee (or mentor) is wildly successful, confident, and has a lot of ego, that is not necessarily a bad thing. Personality traits aren't for you to judge or diminish.

Some of the most successful people I've met have large egos because they have earned their success. There's a difference between having a high self-esteem, pouring into your kids, developing a strong ego, and arrogance. Often people who are arrogant have a low self-esteem, but that's not what we are talking about here. We are talking about not being intimidated by any sort of ego or confidence in your mentor or mentee!

Regardless of which side of the fence you fall on, focus on developing yourself, and you will in turn develop others. Build self-esteem and focus less on how people are perceiving you and judging you. If you're a mentor, use this guide to be even better than you already are. You will face a lot of different personalities, from those who are self-conscious to those who are extremely confident.

Pour into everyone, offer your wisdom and leadership advice, and be a trusted advisor.

Remember that the higher your self-esteem, the more confident you are to take risks and to lead well.

It is our hope that as you study this guidebook, you can learn and grow even more, just as we have.

> *Remember that the higher your self-esteem, the more confident you are to take risks and to lead well.*

At the time of this writing, Tammy coaches 24 university students and several executives and is a Vistage chair with a CEO group in Dallas.

These leaders have companies worth millions and gather to discover best practices and grow their businesses in a confidential setting.

I advise the leaders of many companies across the globe, and I'm also an investor in many winning companies, such as Dogtopia, which began from just an idea and expanded to hundreds of locations.

Tammy was with me and Peter Thomas in Canada on his yacht one day, when a lady showed up discussing Dogtopia. It has since accelerated in size to over 300 locations across North America.

On that day and in the middle of the bay in Canada, Tammy had flown in to facilitate conversations about legacy and life lessons, for a book. In one day, she and Peter and I created the life-changing book *Business Ground Rules*.

You have likely heard and studied many different leadership concepts throughout your life and perhaps you've even experienced different leadership personalities. This book that you're reading today is about how to make a commitment to yourself, to become a stronger leader and mentor in order to pay it forward.

For years, I've coached a wow entrepreneur now in Austin, Tony Hartl—just one entrepreneur who is wildly successful and has created what he calls the "Undefeated Tribe," which is the umbrella for all of his Crunch Fitness locations. Tony is a top franchisee of Crunch Fitness, and the author of *Selling Sunshine*, a book for entrepreneurs, showcasing his learnings building Planet Tan.

After years of coaching him personally, he asked if I could be an extension of him to pour our thinking into his people; so year after year, he hired me (and my team) to go into his organization, build videos, build training, and motivate his people on mindset and my methodology that super-drives results-*Clarity, Focus, and Execution.*

We extended the mentor relationship to the organization, and it's been so much fun along the way.

I have mentored a ton of different people, I've also had many great mentors in my life. (So thankful for this) One of them is an extremely successful entrepreneur . When I asked him, "Why do you still mentor me for free year after year?" he said, "You take action more than anyone I've ever met."

And I want to encourage you as you read this guide to remember excellence along the way; and remember to take action, which will then demonstrate to those you mentor how to do the same.

I am someone who thinks fast and takes action. These are some of my strengths as a coach and a mentor.

When I'm being mentored myself by Jay Rodgers, a wise older man whom I also consider my very close friend, I emphasize results by following up on everything that was said. I want my mentor to understand that I was listening. After any meeting I have, I follow up within hours on all the things my mentors recommended— bullet point by bullet point. Nobody does that that I know of. I know he appreciates it, and it helps cement a special relationship of trust.

I want to encourage you as you read this guide to remember excellence along the way

Are you ready?

Yes, you are. Remember my coined truism— *Production Before Perfection.*

"Leaders lead leaders."

A GREAT MENTOR CAN TRANSFORM LIVES

Mentors change lives.

One great mentor can offer encouragement, wisdom, and practical advice that will often challenge somcone's limiting beliefs and promote lasting change and growth.

Finding a great mentor is essential, and it's an honor both to have one and to be one.

What is a mentor?

A mentor is essentially a **leader** in life and business who has a gift for listening and understanding, and a desire to help others with their personal and business growth.

Congratulations! If you have stepped into the role of mentor, you are viewed as a trusted advisor; and you have the honor and opportunity to help someone on their journey to growth and personal development.

A mentor may mentor someone older, younger, or the same age and may guide someone regarding character traits, life skills, or a business path with practical or philosophical advice. A mentor must establish a structure, cadence, and plan, and must understand what mentorship is not as well.

Mentorship is a gift!

This booklet was created to support you in your mentorship journey. No matter how long you've been a leader, personal development is a day-by-day process. Mentors are committed to personal development and to mentoring others so they will grow, develop, become mentors themselves, and perhaps even outgrow their mentors one day.

This guide is designed to help both experienced and first-time mentors gain clarity about the process of mentorship. Feel free to print this guide and bring it with you to your mentorship sessions. It outlines a clear structure for mentorship.

*A mentor is essentially a **leader** in life and business who has a gift for listening and understanding, and a desire to help others with their personal and business growth.*

What Mentors Are Not
1. Teachers
2. Therapists
3. Life Coaches
4. Parents
5. Best Friends
6. Professors
7. Preachers

Although a mentor's role may touch the edges of many of the roles listed above, it is important to note that it is **not** your responsibility to be a teacher, a parent, or a professor; and it is not appropriate to offer unsolicited teaching moments as if you are teaching a curriculum.

A mentor is a trusted guide, sounding board, active listener, supporter, and cheerleader in someone's life. A mentor stance is available, open, caring and professional.

See how this may contrast with the role of a coach? A hired athletic coach, for instance, or the coach of a football team, as an example, may demonstrate traits that oppose the role of a mentor. It is not uncommon for high school coaches to be focused on discipline and accountability for instance. As a mentor, you should not be concerned about disciplining anyone. Mentorship sessions are leader to leader, despite any imbalances in leadership experience.

Remember that great mentors operate from the mindset that everyone is a leader, and a lifelong learner.

It is important to understand how the role of an athletic coach, or even a life coach, differs from the role of a mentor. A mentor is a trusted and committed all-in guide.

A mentee should be encouraged to come to the mentor with any life, career, or business question or issue that is on their mind and heart.

A mentor should not be in the same role as any kind of coach with a disciplinary or accountability mindset. A mentor is, first and foremost, a peaceful and trusted leader.

A mentor is a trusted and committed all-in guide.

A mentor is not defined by their bank account, their success, or rank in any position. There are many mentors who have not built, created, or sold companies or risen through the ranks of corporate America, but are still gifted in leadership and mentoring others. A mentor is a strategist who can actively listen, observe, process, and then offer wisdom or guidance to the mentee.

MENTORS ARE LEADERS

If you've accepted a mentorship role, you're a leader.

And it's important to make sure you understand that distinction, no matter what role you've actually performed in your career.

Leaders lead.

And that means there's always someone watching and eager to follow. It is a leader's job to consider what a leader is, to read books on leadership and self development, and to understand the process of actively listening. A leader is not a dictator or teacher, but an individual who desires to serve others in order to make an organization, the individual, or the world, a better place.

Think of it this way: If you lead and mentor others, you are increasing their knowledge, wisdom, and self-awareness and investing in a human life. Ideally, the individual will experience growth in some way, pay it forward, and become a stronger and better human themselves.

A leader strives for peace and holistic growth, meaning that he or she understands what the definition of success is, and that it's not merely a financial measuring stick. Success is defined by legacy, by the impact one leaves on this world, and by the way an individual has served others.

A great mentor understands that success is not a comparison with others in their industry or career path and helps their mentee understand that same foundational principal.

It is not the mentor's position to call out mistakes in scheduling or accountability, or to be a disciplinarian. It is not a mentor's role to be a professor, preacher, or coach. A mentor is a leader by very definition because all leaders should give back to others in order to help other leaders grow and develop. Some mentors only focus on youth mentorship, or perhaps college students, while other mentors are focused on leading leaders of all ages.

A great mentor understands that success is not a comparison with others

Think of your role as a mentor as the trusted advisor!

It's an honor to listen without responding and to offer advice when necessary. (However, it may not always be necessary.)

The role of a mentor as a respected and trusted leader and someone the mentee can count on is just as important as the advice given.

LESSON #3

GREAT MENTORS FOCUS ON CONNECTION OVER CORRECTION

If you've ever played high-school sports or any kind of organized sport, you may be familiar with an aggressive and perhaps even outdated coaching style.

One of the humans that I (TK) have mentored for the last couple of years is a college student who was a star on the collegiate hockey team until his mother died. Although he played D1 hockey, this particular school did not offer athletic scholarships;

and he wasn't able to get the financial support to graduate.

There was a lot to process, and it was so fresh that he was still navigating the loss, a lot of anger and grief, and confusion about losing his entire identity as a hockey player. He had played hockey since he was a child. I knew there were no easy answers; however, I also knew that he had to support himself.

All we could do in this situation was to control the controllables, so I mentored him through his next steps and opened his mind to a different career.

We focused on downloading an app that would help him study for his real estate exam quickly in order to get his license and start selling houses. However, this idea only came after talking to him about his goals and interests in life. He had been raised to play hockey; however, he didn't like the culture side of hockey, and specifically the way the coaches had led the teams. Throughout his life, he had many different coaches; and as he explained their tactics, discipline, words, and actions, it became apparent that none of these coaches were what I would consider leaders. The other hockey players, and even my mentee, may disagree; however, a leader doesn't bully, intimidate, or even have to drop F bombs in order to get their point across.

How many times have we seen a high-school coach get reprimanded for that very thing? Coaching and mentorship are roles under the umbrella of leadership. Just like parenting, if you have to hit, use physical or verbal violence, or try to manipulate or intimidate, you're not leading. You're just bullying.

People who intimidate may be coaches, but they are sure not mentors or leaders, and this is a distinction worth mentioning.

When we mentor someone, no matter their age, we do not have to criticize whether they arrived on time, whether they looked professional, or even how they put into action the advice we've given.

> *People who intimidate may be coaches, but they are sure not mentors or leaders*

People who think that's mentorship have it all wrong.

I've learned a lot from watching other so-called leaders attempt to give advice. One had a rather large mentorship organization he had created, and he spent a lot of time mentoring people. He charged for this, but he always had some form of intimidation attached to the mentoring session. Let me explain. This specific entrepreneur had made millions, and because of that had the respect of many. But he didn't have mine. He asked me to meet him at lunch one day and proceeded to drink an entire bottle of wine by himself and then opened another. I looked at his assistant, and I said, "Please take his car keys away so you can drive us back to the office."

She agreed that she would because his advanced age plus two bottles of wine would not be a logical combination .

When we got to the car after lunch, I got in the passenger side; and she abruptly handed him his keys and allowed him to drive us to his office. I was furious!

Obviously, we made it safely, but she was so intimidated by his presence that she could not even take a logical leadership step; in fact, his own employee had no leadership skills herself.

He called me a week later and asked me to lunch, and I said, "I'm not going to meet with you unless you let me drive." I told him I would meet him, but that I was coming from my office across town and would meet him at the restaurant, which was in the middle. It made absolutely no sense to go to his office.

"No, I'm not going to meet with you unless you ride with me, and I will drive," he insisted.

I received no less than six calls in the coming weeks from his assistant to set up a lunch meeting, and each time she told me to come to the office first. Each time I said I would meet him at the restaurant, and each time he declined.

He left me a voicemail and said that if I didn't trust him to drive, he wouldn't be meeting with me; and I said, "Well, then you won't be meeting with me."

He attempted to manipulate and intimidate me into a mentorship situation, which is not good leadership. I point this out to show you that there is a difference between the title of a doctor and a doctor who is actually good. There is a difference between the title of a mentor (because anyone can give themselves that title) and a solid mentor.

Mentors do not talk just about themselves.

Mentors want to change lives.

The mentor does not come to the session with pre-prepared life lessons. A mentor comes to each session with a mentor mindset.

What is a mentor mindset?

The mentor mindset is:

- Open-minded
- Actively listens
- "them"-focused, not "me"-focused
- Has no pre-prepared slides or lesson
- Resists the urge to refer back to their life or experiences—talking about themselves
- Open-hearted
- Cautious and clear communicator
- Professional

Many times a mentor will be tempted to refer to their own path. However, every individual is unique; and it's important to meet people where they are and mentor them to their next desired step. A mentee may come to you with a perceived problem or some sort of issue they need to untangle.

Be aware that the meeting may go differently than you had planned, and be willing to pivot and address the issue at hand. This means you must stop talking. You must always listen and create space for your mentee to open up. This only occurs when a foundation of trust is built.

Trust occurs after consistent communication or text in between meetings, and with being actively involved in replying to the one you mentor. Often times mentoring occurs more in the in between— the weeks between any actual, defined face-to-face mentoring sessions.

Be responsive, and always be encouraging.

Learn to communicate with the person you are mentoring the way they prefer to communicate— not the way you prefer to communicate. Remember that mentors are leaders, and it's important to take the lead.

Be professional, don't look for things they're doing wrong in relating or communicating to you, and understand that it's a gift to be a mentor.

.

ADOPT A MENTOR STANCE

A mentor stance means showing up as a leader. It's adopting an active understanding of maintaining a professional demeanor; communication style; and method of scheduling, meeting, and relating to the ones you're leading.

Iron sharpens iron, and your mentee is a leader themselves, ready to set the world on fire! It doesn't matter if they are 21 or 61, you are in a position to breathe life into this individual for a short period of time; and it's important to maintain a mentor stance.

You are not a boss or a best friend, and there's no need to impress or feel as if you have to offer homework or a report card. Think of it as a conversation with leaders.

Having a mentor stance means you must resist the urge to talk often, and instead become a facilitator who listens. Ideally you'll help your leader mentee come to conclusions on their own through affirmation and active listening.

A mentor is not there to tell the individual mentee everything about themselves (mentor) or their career path, nor are they there to preach or teach.

As tempting as it is to answer the question, "So, how did you get your start?" in depth, it's important to answer it succinctly; and while the dialogue and communication are necessary, it's much more important to allow the mentee to talk about whatever is on their heart or mind.

Talk about yourself when asked or as an introduction, but make sure you're always focused on allowing your mentee to talk, vent, or ask questions.

It's much more important to allow the mentee to talk about whatever is on their heart or mind.

To give you an idea of the appropriate conversational mix, a mentor should talk 20 percent of the time in general and the mentee 80 percent.

The ideal mentor will actively listen to their mentee and understand that each mentorship session is an individual, separate session and not a continuation of the last one. Why is this important?

In one mentorship session, you may have identified a problem the mentee is struggling with. You may have discussed this problem; however, it doesn't mean that your mentee wants to carry on that discussion next time. Each mentorship session should be viewed as a brand new moment; and the mentor should pause, think, listen, and consider any new needs of their mentee.

For clarity on this concept, think about a moment when you may have discussed a personal issue as a young teenager or a young person with your parent. Or perhaps you discussed it with a friend or family member who then brought up the same distressing issue again weeks or months later.

Don't revive issues from your last mentorship session.

They are there for encouragement and coaching, not counseling and accountability. Open each session as a completely new opportunity to sit face-to-face and hear what your mentee has to say.

UNDERSTAND MENTORSHIP PERSONALITIES!

There are many different types of mentorship personalities. We highlight this to allow you to take a look at which one you think you might be, in order to reflect and increase   your self-awareness.

Do you need to make some changes? Maybe you do, or maybe you don't.

In discovering mentorship personalities, it's also important to state that a mentor and mentee do not have to necessarily be like minded. Tony and I have very different perspectives; yet when we coach each other every December prior to the new year, we both walk away with transforming wins.

If you bounced all of your ideas, off of someone who was exactly like you I don't think there would be much growth. Alignment is comfortable, but disruption can take you places you never thought you could go.

One thing that Tony taught me is *Production Before Perfection* (**PBP**), and I applied this principle of speed to publishing.

When I first heard the term *Production Before Perfection,* I was horrified because as an author and a trained journalism major, you don't allow imperfection. A book is part of your legacy, and it's going to be out there in cyberspace and on bookshelves and even in grandma's attic for a long time. A book is going to transfer throughout generations.

I was focused on quality and not quantity. So initially our perspectives were very different. Tony has published over 100 books, whereas I had focused only on big name-brand publishers and books that took time and intellectual thought to create.

In the past, I had written books that sold to major publishing companies and had acquired publishing contracts upwards of six figures. One book is being optioned by a major television studio as a series!

You do not have to think exactly the same as your mentors and as a mentor, you do not have to coach others who only want to follow in your footsteps or career path. Ultimately, it's your core principles and not your résumé that are going to help with leadership development.

You can learn more from someone who has achieved great things far differently than you have than you can learn from someone who has walked your exact same journey. The differences in your personality and perspectives can be magical and transforming as you each engage in conversation.

Things mentors do subconsciously:
- Do you tend to talk a lot?
- Do you tend to tell people what to do instead of actively listening for what they need?
- Do you tend to offer the same tools to fit completely different human problems?

If so, it may be time to grow as a mentor.

Here are a few examples of the various types of mentors.

1. The Problem Solver

    The problem-solver mentor is a natural-born problem solver and often can't sleep unless they solve a problem first. This personality type may look for problems and feel as if they are not contributing to the mentor relationship if there are none.

    It is important for this problem-solver type personality to understand that your mentee may not have a problem to solve.

    However, your mentee may remember conversations, lessons, or connections you had years later when it is time for them to mentor someone else.

2. The Preacher Mentor

    Oftentimes, advice, even when well-intended, can come across as forceful or preachy. A strong mentor with a background in leadership will need to sharpen the skill of active listening to be a valuable mentor. A mentor who comes across as preachy will have strong opinions and belief systems that may appear rigid.

This type of mentor may have a subliminal agenda to preach or teach specific items that are on their heart. They are often well-meaning, yet they infuse every answer with a specific agenda. It is important to listen as a mentor to the belief systems, style, and communication cadence of your mentee.

As a mentor, you can freely share your feelings and beliefs when you have developed a comfortable relationship and conversational style with your mentee.

3. The Best-Friend Mentor

Some mentors are driven by a need to be viewed positively and as a soft place to fall. While all of these personality styles are natural traits for many people, it's important to identify that, as a mentor, your role is to be available, trustworthy, and caring.

It is not our role to become best friends. You are another resource in your mentee's life to help them grow.

Positive and Ideal Mentor Skills:
The ideal mentor has the following skills and actively works on their own personal growth and leadership.

1. Active listener
2. Listens to understand
3. Listens without interrupting
4. Listens for needs, unresolved issues, pain, or things left unsaid.
5. Asks questions before offering advice
6. Asks, "How can I help you in your life?" or "How's your heart?" or "How are you feeling today?"
7. Pauses before responding
8. Responds with care and integrity
9. Has a high degree of emotional intelligence
10. Resists the urge to teach or impose views
11. Prioritizes connection over correction
12. Communicates based on how their mentee prefers versus how they prefer (e.g., text over calls)

LESSON #6
STAY ORGANIZED AND APPROACHABLE

Much of what the people you lead learn will come from the way you live your own life through your scheduling, organization, and encouragement. Often people remember the encourager more than they remember the person who taught them several lessons at work. But they will also remember how you showed up.

This guide will help both experienced and new mentors understand how to sharpen your skills and

29

serves as a reminder of the important traits and actions of a mentor.

Now is not the time to prove yourself, or verbally list all of your accomplishments. You've already achieved the highest position one can achieve as a leader and that is the position of a mentor. There is not another title that is more noble, nor one that requires such intentionality both prior to meeting with someone and post meeting, than the role of a trusted advisor.

But what if I'm not equipped?

Two words: you are!

It's important to step back and identify that imposter syndrome is real, and even the greatest CEOs I've ever worked with have told me that they wrestle with it. Imposter syndrome hits the ultra wealthy and successful when they feel as if they may be entering an area of uncertainty in which they don't have experience or competence.

It is important to note that wealth, business experience, running a company, or working successfully within a corporate environment do not equip a person for mentorship.

A mentor has a unique skill set! A mentor is a leader leading a leader.

Mentorship is an entirely new and different role and requires a completely different mindset than many business leaders are accustomed to!

But what if I'm not equipped? Two words: you are!

Know Before You Go

The number one tool to having successful face-to-face mentorship sessions is preparation. Create a binder with your mentee's name on it and keep any notes and personal information inside that binder.

But, don't bring it to the first meeting. Go to the first meeting just open-minded and empty-handed—and that includes your phone.

Prepare before you go, and be extremely intentional about what you will say, what you will wear, and how you will listen.

Spend time in prayer prior to each and every session and ask God for specific wisdom regarding your time with your mentee. It may be a time of rest and listening, or it may be a moment to offer advice or intervene in an emotional issue or question. Pray in advance and clear your mind, schedule, and heart.

ELIMINATE ALL ASSUMPTIONS ABOUT YOUR MENTEE

Imagine what would happen if we acted on all of the assumptions we had about others without getting to know them. It's easy to Google someone these days and think you know them; but you will have greater success if you eliminate all assumptions about people, including the ones you're going to lead and mentor.

Often times people will surprise you in many ways. Let them!

So leave your assumptions behind; and when you have that initial mentorship meeting, make sure you know how to arrive, that you put your phone away, and that you have some sort of structure in your mind even as you understand that you're also going to be actively listening to the person you're talking to.

One way to break the ice is to bring a connection tool with you to your first meeting.

CONNECTION TOOL

Bring a book to give your mentee as a gift. This book can be your favorite leadership book, a book that someone gave you, or a book that you would just like to give your mentee as a gift.

The following is a sample structure for your mentorship sessions:

- **Setting:** A neutral setting such as a coffee shop or restaurant.
- **Table:** Eliminate your phone from view prior to your mentee's arrival. Read a book or just sit and wait.
- **Mentor stance:** Maintain a calm, clear, unhurried stance. Leave your problems at the office or home and do not allow mental, physical, or phone distractions to enter your time together.

Session 1: Connection

In this session, set the groundwork for a mentor mindset by establishing a professional stance, yet with a relaxed demeanor. Show up for the session unhurried, and arrive in advance. Do not schedule your first session in between meetings, and do not bring your worldly activities or chaos, which we all have, into the session.

Schedule your session at a neutral, comfortable place, such as a Starbucks or a local restaurant.

Make sure to ask your mentee in advance: "What's your favorite coffee shop or restaurant?" Choose a location that is neutral. Do not choose your home or office space.

In session one, take a deep breath, smile, and make a point to only focus on one thing: connection.

Even if your mentee asks all about you, make a point of talking about your mentee and asking questions about their life.

Communication style: Light, joyful, fun, relaxed, professional.

Conversation: 80 percent mentee talks, 20 percent mentor talks

This is important because it can be easy to talk about ourselves. After all, it's natural! But the best way to establish a connection with your mentee is to ask them simple questions, not difficult questions, about their life.

Open-ended questions such as, "So, tell me about yourself?" will get the ball rolling.

Other questions can center on their day, their week, or even their last vacation. "So, tell me something about the last trip you took? Where was it?"

You could also ask your mentee about their family, school, or what they're most excited about in life.

Remember that this first session is not about providing advice. It is only about trust and connection. Building trust is a very important foundational building block of mentorship. Trust only comes through clarity, communication, and consistency.

BE CONSISTENT

Consistency builds trust; and there are many different ways you can build trust with those you lead, including maintaining your agreed-to Zoom schedule, conference call time, or face-to-face meeting location. Consistency also can be created through weekly text messages, where you text your mentor on a specific day. Scheduling these items on your calendar are important to maintain consistency and build trust.

If you've already had your first session with your mentee, one of the ways you can maintain consistency is by meeting at a similar location in session two, whether it's your own office or somewhere with less distractions.

In session two, it is important to remain consistent, and if possible, meet at the exact same spot you had identified previously (as long as that's working for your mentee). A consistent location brings comfort and trust, and you can develop a consistent cadence online, too.

If you're establishing mentorship calls or a Zoom meeting versus a face-to-face meeting due to location challenges, create consistency by setting up four weeks of calls in advance on the same day at the same time. Make sure you are a flexible mentor and allow your mentee to reschedule without questions. Remember, you are not their soccer coach, volleyball coach, or teacher. It is not your job to reprimand, discipline, or hold them accountable.

It is an honor to be a mentor; and in that role, you are a trusted guide in life and business to help them on their journey of self-development and growth.

Meetup Locations

The extraordinary mentor has enough emotional intelligence to understand that the spot the mentee chooses may not be the mentor's favorite. Select something that is not difficult to travel to for your mentee.

It is an honor to be a mentor

Think through this process and know before you go if you are, in fact, going to meet your mentee face-to-face. Make it make sense, and make it easy for your mentee.

Although it may be tempting to switch up the location and be adventurous, consistency creates trust; and you can create a consistent meeting spot by ensuring that you select a location your mentee prefers.

Meet at that location for your second session as well, and it will be your consistent meetup spot.

In session two, you can dig deeper than in session one. Open with 10 to 15 minutes of casual conversation while maintaining your relaxed yet professional mentorship stance.

Do not arrive with a notebook, and do not record your sessions. This is not a job interview. Above all else, have fun and let your personality shine through!

In this session, your role is that of a warm, professional, and personal sounding board. Your mentee may have questions on their mind to ask you about their industry, career path, or personal problems. Let them know that you are open to any discussion.

Actively listen to their question.

In session two, your goal should be to actively listen and facilitate openness and a discussion about anything that is on their mind or heart.

In this session, you can feel free to ask the question: "Is there any life or business issue that you're dealing with this week?"

And you can wait for your mentee to bring up whatever is on their mind. Don't be surprised if it's a simple personal issue about getting their car registered, a relationship, bills, how to handle a problem at work with a coworker, or even any other small problem creating mental clutter in their life.

Actively listen, engage, and encourage helpful conversation. You know what to do! Be yourself and provide leadership.

Session Follow-up:
A strong mentor responds to a mentee within four hours of a text, phone call, or email, if possible. Establish this response rate of communication up front as a standard. This is between you and yourself and will build trust.

Understand that the questions a mentee may have may arise in the follow-up.

You can set boundaries; but understand that as a mentor, you have a responsibility to be open and available to your mentee. If a question arises in a text or follow-up email, respond accordingly. Do not brush them off, and say, "We will talk about this in our next mentorship session."

LESSON #9
FOLLOW UP

Follow up consistently and remember the four C's of mentorship: Clarity, Communication, Commitment, and Consistency.

Think about it as a **relationship** that you are developing much like you would any other relationship that's important to you.

You wouldn't *not* follow up or *not* respond to or *not* actively text someone you wanted to be in a relationship with, whether it was a love relationship, a friendship, or even a client.

If you don't actively reach out and communicate on a weekly basis, there's a risk that someone else might. Think about this relationship in the same way, and understand that your mentor will not always be the one initiating communication.

A simple method of communication is a simple text asking them about their week or how they're doing.

Follow-up is critical
The things that happen in between mentorship sessions are often more important than what happens in a mentorship session. If you establish that your mentee can text you, he or she may text you just prior to an important interview.

Be responsive, and reply as soon as possible. It is an honor to be a mentor and to pour into someone's life. Oftentimes, people end up valuing their mentors and becoming entwined with their families and lives.

Build trust by being consistent and responsive in your communications.

Respond in text or email and communicate clearly. It is not uncommon for someone to think about their mentorship session and have a deeper understanding, self-awareness, revelation, or follow-up message after your session. Sometimes this occurs weeks later; other times it may occur an hour later.

The things that happen in between mentorship sessions are often more important than what happens in a mentorship session.

Be responsive in order to build trust! But you don't have to be perfect!

Mentors are often mentors for life, not just within that one-hour session. When you sign up to be a mentor, you are making a conscious, willing decision to be in someone's life for a short time or even longer. And that's a commitment.

REFINE YOUR COMMUNICATION SKILLS

Mentorship can help individuals develop a variety of key skills, such as communication, active listening, and understanding. It's a process of strengthening. As we said earlier, iron sharpens iron; and it's a beautiful journey because as you are mentoring, someone else, you are also increasing your awareness and understanding.

Understanding comes when you mentor someone in a completely different industry with completely different goals and perhaps even someone that is a very different personality type.

This only strengthens you as a leader.

An excellent mentor views mentorship as a way to refine and develop their communication skills.

1. **Mentorship** encourages open dialogue, enhancing both verbal and non-verbal communication abilities. Mentees learn to effectively articulate their thoughts and ideas. They also tend to ask a lot of questions, and this gives you the chance to develop your answers and observations after actively listening.

2. **Leadership Skills:** Through mentorship, individuals can develop their leadership capabilities by observing and practicing effective leadership behaviors and strategies demonstrated by their mentors. Taking a mentee on a vision-board session, actively helping them set their goals, or allowing them to shadow you at work is one way for them to be exposed to different types of leadership.

3. **Problem-Solving Skills:** Mentors should listen first, before offering any solutions and problem-solving.

4. **Emotional Intelligence:** Mentorship relationships foster self-awareness and

empathy, helping mentees improve their emotional intelligence, which is essential for effective interpersonal interactions.

5. **Networking Skills:** Mentees learn how to build and maintain professional relationships, enhancing their networking abilities and increasing their access to opportunities.

6. **Goal-Setting and Planning:** Mentorship encourages individuals to set professional goals and create actionable plans to achieve them, fostering a sense of accountability and purpose.

7. **Time Management:** Working with a mentor can help mentees learn how to prioritize tasks and manage their time effectively, balancing multiple responsibilities.

8. **Adaptability and Resilience:** Mentors often share their experiences in overcoming challenges, which helps mentees develop resilience and learn to adapt to changing circumstances.

Becoming a great mentor helps individuals cultivate a range of skills that are essential for personal and professional development, and grows your skills at the same time.

PRACTICE ACTIVE LISTENING

We save the best for last because active listening is different than just listening, and it plays a vital role in building trust during your meetings in several ways:

When participants actively listen, it shows that they value the speaker's thoughts and opinions. This respect fosters a sense of being heard and understood. This is a tool that involves a lot of discipline and self-control in order to listen to someone else without jumping in, interrupting, and providing the answers.

Listening versus Active Listening

The way that we as humans listen to others in a conversation has been naturally degraded by unnatural forces such as that phone we hold in our hand. Technology is great; yet the way it impacts our processing and attention span has changed us. Today we are all accustomed to receiving our content in 30 or 60 second reels; and because of that, we are used to multitasking and looking at our phones while also listening to someone else.

However, in mentorship, it requires a different type of listening, which is likely to feel forced due to the way we have been programmed to live.

By feeling forced, we hope to create an awareness that active listening is a skill to develop. It is no different than dressing for success, versus putting on a comfortable sweatshirt and jeans. When you go to the office, you may be allowed to dress as casually as you want due to a relaxed dress code, but you may also want to stand out by dressing for success wearing business attire.

No one ever lost credibility by overdressing in a professional situation.

Listening is a process of learning how to focus. Mentorship is about leveraging your knowledge and skills, but one of those skills is extreme focus. It's very hard to mentor someone if you do not have eye contact and have not developed active listening skills.

Passive listening is what we do every day in our day-to-day lives.

Listening is a process of learning how to focus.

Active listeners create an environment where others feel confident sharing their ideas and concerns. This openness is essential for fostering a connection and building mutual trust.

This type of listening involves a lot of silence.

If there's a break in the conversation, active listening involves recapping what the other person has said in some authentic way, asking questions, and summarizing what has been said.

This behavior ensures clarity, shows engagement, and allows for misunderstandings to be addressed promptly.

When you consistently practice active listening, it signals that you are dependable and committed to understanding others. This reliability enhances trustworthiness.

Have you ever had a time where you felt misunderstood?

Create a space for communication that offers so much clarity that there can be no misunderstanding with the person you're mentoring or with other people in any kind of meeting. Active listening, as well as all the principles within this guide, will make you a better communicator in every setting.

Active listening allows for differing viewpoints to be considered, which can minimize conflicts and increase cooperation.

ABOUT THE AUTHORS

Tammy King

Tammy Kling is a Vistage Chair, leading at the world's largest CEO organization. She is the founder of The Conversation, an annual event for CEOs, speakers, and entrepreneurs.

The goal of The Conversation is to equip world changers through deep and interactive discussions about relevant life issues, such as legacy, blind spots and intentionality.

Her TEDx platform and company, Voices Speakers Bureau, is designed to equip world changers by multiplying their message.

Kling often provides consulting, speakers, and organizational facilitators to corporations that are facing a merger or in need of a vibrant leader for a conference.

As an expert in communication and crisis management, Kling helps organizations navigate uncertain, black swan events. Her background as a crisis management leader, working airplane crashes for a major airline, established the foundation for a future of coaching leaders.

A popular television company has just optioned the rights to her book, to create a television series.

ABOUT THE AUTHORS

Tony Jeary

Tony Jeary - The RESULTS Guy™ has impacted people's success now for over thirty years. Like a top professional athlete preparing for competition, Tony takes each assignment, engagement, and/or partnership with extreme seriousness. Tony likes to win, and he wins by helping others win.

He chooses carefully the people and organizations he works with and then goes all in, focusing on what will provide the highest/next-level return on effort.

Tony is a prolific author, with most of his titles (over one hundred books!) focused on helping others get *RESULTS Faster*! He and his team work mainly in his unique, private RESULTS Center, located just a few minutes north of DFW Airport, which houses his thirty-plus years of best practices, courses, and tools.

He is blessed with an awesome family whom he loves on, prays for, and nourishes daily. His friendships are many; he thrives on making their lives better. He's an encourager to the world and is committed to an ever-growing Rolodex that numbers in the tens of thousands.

He loves partnering with the successful who want to supercharge their visions and make them reality even faster.

NOTES